Ponds

The Poiema Poetry Series

Poems are windows into worlds; windows into beauty, goodness, and truth; windows into understandings that won't twist themselves into tidy dogmatic statements; windows into experiences. We can do more than merely peer into such windows; with a little effort we can fling open the casements, and leap over the sills into the heart of these worlds. We are also led into familiar places of hurt, confusion, and disappointment, but we arrive in the poet's company. Poetry is a partnership between poet and reader, seeking together to gain something of value—to get at something important.

Ephesians 2:10 says, "We are God's workmanship..." *poiema* in Greek—the thing that has been made, the masterpiece, the poem. The Poiema Poetry Series presents the work of gifted poets who take Christian faith seriously, and demonstrate in whose image we have been made through their creativity and craftsmanship.

These poets are recent participants in the ancient tradition of David, Asaph, Isaiah, and John the Revelator. The thread can be followed through the centuries—through the diverse poetic visions of Dante, Bernard of Clairvaux, Donne, Herbert, Milton, Hopkins, Eliot, R. S. Thomas, and Denise Levertov—down to the poet whose work is in your hand. With the selection of this volume you are entering this enduring tradition, and as a reader contributing to it.

—D.S. Martin
Series Editor

Ponds

J. C. Scharl

CASCADE *Books* • Eugene, Oregon

PONDS

Copyright © 2024 J. C. Scharl. All rights reserved. Except for brief quotations in critical publications or reviews, no part of this book may be reproduced in any manner without prior written permission from the publisher. Write: Permissions, Wipf and Stock Publishers, 199 W. 8th Ave., Suite 3, Eugene, OR 97401.

Cascade Books
An Imprint of Wipf and Stock Publishers
199 W. 8th Ave., Suite 3
Eugene, OR 97401

www.wipfandstock.com

PAPERBACK ISBN: 979-8-3852-1064-0
HARDCOVER ISBN: 979-8-3852-1065-7
EBOOK ISBN: 979-8-3852-1066-4

Cataloguing-in-Publication data:

Names: Scharl, Jane Clark. | author.

Title: Ponds / Jane Clark Scharl.

Description: Eugene, OR: Cascade Books, 2024 | Series: The Poiema Poetry Series

Identifiers: ISBN 979-8-3852-1064-0 (paperback) | ISBN 979-8-3852-1065-7 (hardcover) | ISBN 979-8-3852-1066-4 (ebook)

Subjects: LCSH: Poetry. | Christian poetry.

Classification: PS301 S32 2024 (paperback) | PS301 2024 (ebook)

04/01/24

To Scott, with love

Contents

Reflection	1
After the Funeral	2
Saint January	3
New Year's Morning	5
Salt	6
Philosopher's Millstone	7
Pomegranate	8
Candles	9
Spring Evening	14
The Newlywed	15
Abraham Barters with God	17
Relics	18
Annunciation	20
The Widow of Cana	21
Sestina for Mother	23
The Trout	25
Collect: Pebbles on the Beach by the Puget Sound	26
Daybreak in Bretagne	28
Post Partum	29
Act of Poetry	31
White Lily	32
The New House	34
To My Unborn Child	36

Church Cleaning	37
Watercolor	39
The Circle	40
Harvesting Olives in Arcadia	41
Hymn to an Open Box of Spaghetti as It Falls from the Pantry Shelf	42
The School of Athens in the Sonoran Desert	43
Overflow	44
Marco Polo	45
Resurrection After a Headache	46
Icon of Elijah in the Wilderness	47
The Fig	49
Leap	50
Sonnet for Early Autumn	51
In the Sandbox	52
Making Peace with the Cat	54
Still Life with Dead Jackdaw	55
My Children Gather Acorns	56
Penelope	57
The Lark Ascending Over Phoenix	59
Explanation	61
Words and Pictures	62
Down the Basement Stairs	64
Winter Scene	65
Part	66
Ponds	68
Evening Meditation	72
Acknowledgements	73

Reflection

Leaves this morning are young moons,
flashing with a glow that is not their own,
tossing borrowed bits of color
back to the visible world.

Watching them, I wonder
about all the other light,
the unseen illuminations that slip,
too quick to be seen, down through the skin

of the world to its heart, where maybe
there lie halls of long still rooms
where things can rest, and not reflect,
and where I cannot go.

After the Funeral

for Mom

So that is all life is: a darkening trail;
a coin once flipped and idly caught again;
a former lover's final correspondence;
a ruined cathedral; a probing blame-filled glance…

Is that all life is? a clearance sale?
a fire gone out? a broken useless pen?
the silence that always follows a sentence?
a scattered rose? a sigh? a squandered chance?

Yet—evening reflections on the pond,
and purple-veiled icons at Lent. Feeble
winter sunlight strengthens. Tiny sandals
by the door. A house tidied. Beyond
the playhouse, a tree planted. The smallest evil
mended. In the dark, pinpricks of candles.

Saint January

I.

New Year's Eve: we poor godlings
huddle around tinsel fires
that don't warm our hands.

The West's a cauldron
of clouds. The sunset rises

like smoke. In the temple
of Janus, the war-doors
are always open now.

II.

I know, I know,
the girl shakes her head,
reaching for the cigarettes.

*It's not midnight yet. I promised
myself this'll be my year.*

The girl is everywhere. Everywhere
such drugstore lips tick,
counting down.

III.

Everywhere the world's moving
through its stages of decay; it's just
me trying to stay put,

which is to say go backwards,
back to when (in my mind at least)

the world was full of solid things
that cast the shadows
smiting me today.

IV.

St. Januarius died in Napoli
with his companions. Again, a priest
elevates a vial of that congealed blood—

St. Januarius dies in Napoli,
and we, his changeling companions, watch

his blood resolve into bright liquid
and in the tilted glass again,
outside of time, revolve.

New Year's Morning

Rain again last night—ripped
the baby tips off the ends of the acacia—

and now the sky's gray and tight-lipped
over the hard bulk of the mesa.

The new year's coming in cold
today, and silver. Today I am amazed

by existence, by that weary old
sun whose light is really time, glaze-

eyed with travel—today, unbound
briefly, I stand beside that light and see

it, incredulous, watch itself passing all around
those bruised, oracular trees.

Salt

Don't salt your food before you taste it,
my mother used to say.
It might insult the cook—
my mother, keen-eyed little chef
forever serving up those heaping dishes
of her own life, and I,
unthinking, tasteless, salting.

Philosopher's Millstone

Lord, I've lived too long in my mind,
that far-off world that does not exist,
so long I've lost the way back. I've walked
too long beside myself. I've heard
my ears hearing as an echo,
seen my eyes seeing but not what they saw.

Now the rising of the sun pierces me
like the cry of another woman's child,
and light in the morning wakes in me
that which is not mine to soothe.

Oh give me for a soul a sun-sweet apple
heavy with the seeds of this one spring,
or even a kernel of bright wheat
instead of this philosopher's millstone
around my neck, this granite assurance
that will gleam in no world's sun.

Pomegranate

My heart is like a pomegranate
as a simile seems a little simplistic
these days (even the meter beats
too neatly to strike true)
but nonetheless
there's something to it:
how a pomegranate cracks
and bleeds a little when opened,
no matter how gentle your hands
and how a few seeds spill out
like little dreams, smoldering crimson
as coals around their dark core.
How more seeds cling
to the membrane in a strangled
Fibonacci order, so determined
to hold their place that each
is a little misshapen. How
at the deep recesses of the fruit,
so deep it is nearly the bottom,
there is a bad patch,
the underbelly of a faint bruise
on the outer skin,
where a brown ooze festers,
leaking its slow poison.

Candles

In a traditional Tenebrae service,
fourteen candles are extinguished,
leaving only one burning at the close.

I.

With a single votive burning,
in the shadows on the wall I mark
what seems so like
the very melting of time bound
by smoke-dimmed glass. Just now I suspect
Plato was right, and the life of the soul consists
in that motion, that flame
we see receding and cannot grasp.

II.

Shutting off a light is nothing
like pinching out a flame.
The candle yearns to burn. Its flame
wraps round each thrust of air, willing
to struggle, to survive. It parries a blow
and all the room shivers
with purgating shades.
Like so.

III.

Fire's earned an ugly name
as the matter of the pit, but
if Dante'd known the soulless glare
cast by rows of high-watt LEDs,
he might have limned the halls of Hell
with staring bulbs, and done no harm to

either his verse or to his mystic creed,
though perhaps to his current reputation.

IV.

Parmenides, though, would have loved
that stark-white artificial light
cleaving time from space, rendering
our sense of change anachronistic, even
void. Now we need not hear
what sunset tells us, for the world is never dark
and need never become so. Thus
progress becomes stasis, as well as cruel.

V.

So it seems that after all this time
the world's gone flat again, leveled
beneath a spotlight Bosch would jam
up the devil's ass to shine
down on an unaltering land
where all is common and commonly
exposed, and manipulated, machined
past grace of change. So numquam memento mori.

VI.

Illusions of such permanence
illumine nothing of what is
but show only that, despite
the brightness of my nights, no thing
I know can be sustained forever.
In the dark between stars we see
the staggering scale of our ignorance,
the permanence of such illusions.

VII.

Advantages, of course, are legion
to a world no longer thralled to sunrise,
but how then to explain this sense
of—say it—relief that comes
from being somewhere dark, alone?
Imagine a world where quiet
and dark and open spaces become a prize
withheld from those who do not know to take it.

VIII.

And *Tenebrae*: the fifteen candles
on Maundy Thursday afternoon
lit in silence, and in silence
put out (all but one); the readings
from Jeremiah of the mire;
shadows closing in; at last,
clattering kneelers; engloomed we stand;
in conclusion, Our Father (silent).

IX.

Come this day, what can I say?
How can it be anything but good
for us to dwell less often
in the dark? The dark—that dark
from which we come and to which we
stay bound with cords of flesh and bone.
A flame seems to struggle against the breath.
How can this be anything but good?

X.

At home I have a lamp that spits.
I will not have it fixed, for it
cracks like a taper at the shrine

of Rosaline the Incorrupt,
who after seven centuries
still wears no waxen mask. Her eye,
open, enshrined, reflects a light
far off that even in perfect stillness stirs.

XI.

If your eye causes you to sin,
don't hesitate to pluck it out—
sure, it may be better
to enter the Kingdom with one eye
than to burn in Hell with both,
but what about that third alternative:
both scandalous eyes ripped out
so I stumble through Heaven, blind?

XII.

"I am the light of the world," okay,
but please, not the fluorescent tube
of some cosmic office park. Christ,
no. The Lord of the world
marks and hallows His harrowed ones
not with filaments but with flames
and from stark-shattered hell heaves lady Eve
into the dappled light of day.

XIII.

Last night at twilight I looked away
for an instant, and in the west
the darkness clapped down like a bowl
over the earth. Still, in the last
snatch of radiance, close by
there blazed before the dark the coal
of a moth's blood-red underwing, flashing forth
to flame with the very violence of God.

XIV.

On the altar of this world
my soul flickers like a candle
before a tabernacle I cannot see.
The priest has finished praying. The choir
stands. The Mass is ended. The rites
demand, if the body of God is taken
away from here, the candles be extinguished.

O Lord, suffer me not to be put out.

Spring Evening

There are evenings braced
by light like pillars,
when flecks of time
hang in the air
like dust, suspended.
This is one of them.

Even the breeze
is its own calm.
The unending ripples
on the pond
become, by repetition,
a calm beyond stillness.

This, I think, may be
how the world ends:
in a moment
that simply stays,
trembling in place
like an apple blossom,
but forever.

The Newlywed

The myths are wrong—it wasn't Hades' fault.
No one gave me those seeds to eat. I found them
myself one afternoon; in that salted
soil nothing grew except one stem

of pomegranate. The summers there are cruel.
It was the only growing thing I'd seen
in many months. It glistened like a jewel…
Of course I plucked it. It was a little green.

I found it difficult to open by
myself, but when I asked Hades he shook
his head and gave one of those endless sighs
I find so irritating. You see: *I* took

the fruit. No one gave me anything—
I took it. I reached my hand and twisted it
from the dusty branch, and everything
that came with it, I took that too, and bit

the skin to break it, and with my fingers split
it wide and pried those seeds out, one by one.
I took five, and of those, two were bitter.
But three I ate. That's when he knew he'd won,

according to the myths, and crowed in triumph
and all that dead land laughed. That's not what happened
at all. The truth is, he tried to warn me off.
He as good as said it was a trap, and

told me that land's fruit is bitter. I laughed
at him. I think I even offered him a piece,
which he refused, and laughing still I passed
him by and continued up the street,

and it was a little while before I knew
that when I cracked the fruit of that weird land
I felt my heart crack open with a new
grief, not now loss or hate but bland

pity and even, yes, love, blistering
up within me like a welt, love
for those endless streets and houses staggering
beneath the flat and changeless sky above,

for the scrawny bush that twisted as it grew
to bear its stunted fruit, and for the clean
dry light that slaughters and preserves. I knew:
Never would all I loved be whole again.

Abraham Barters with God

One morning after Abraham had bartered so
with God, he arose and went forth lightly
from his tent, and everywhere he saw
dew clinging like a shroud to every limb
of earth, he saw the sky hung low
with cloud, and lifting up his eyes he saw,
rising from the plain below, distant smoke
from two damped pyres like candle-stubs,
and in his heart he felt great grief; he felt a little
sin of pride; but he felt no surprise.

Relics

I.

It's water does this
to wood: petrifies the honeyed grain
so time runs off the light-shot stone like rain
leaving nothing, taking nothing.

Ages back, a river
filled the Painted Desert—see its traces
here, reflected in the fractured silver faces
of the quartz crystals. It's water

does this sometimes—
more often, though, the sodden log, the drift-
caught fraying limb, the tree trunk rift
to molder on the forest floor.

But sometimes, time
strikes a deal with the living, and rather
than bringing rot and ruin, water
stills, and by slow alchemy

renders a single tree
endless. So whole groves melt away
and this one lingers, beyond decay,
kept whole, nothing lost

except everything beside.

II.

Earlier this afternoon the light—
which is time, which is time going by—lay
at its winter angle of repose, and stayed
a little longer than usual, resting

on the blue of a vase,
the yellow of the tulips balanced
above hollow luminous stems, the valiant
colors pushing out to meet

all that apocalypse. And briefly
it teetered on the very limit: the blue
sinking down almost to bottomless, too
infinite to see—the long blue

of Mary's robe—the green
stems trembling like sheer curtains around
columns of rampant life—crowned
with leaping blooms like flame.

Keep it for me, mind: mix lapis
for the vase and verdigris the stems. Leaf
the blooms in gold, the whole sheaf—
even that faded one, hanging upside down

like a ladder from heaven.

Annunciation

Beyond the brimming ages Gabriel waits,
his foremost message burning on his breath.
Through time men slide, creeping through the gates
of birth and out again the doors of death.

He sees kings rise and kingdoms fall to dust;
he sees unnumbered souls unfleshed; to some
he gives slight hints, but the full knowledge must
wait, for his best words are not for them.

Then at last, coming from afar
he sees, gleaming like a golden pin
in time's folds, Mary, rising like a star
above the fretted seas of what had been;

bright hinge on which the gate of Heaven creaks,
to her he turns, inclines himself, and speaks.

The Widow of Cana

Yes, that was me—that was my miracle,
my wedding scene, my tale, though I am scarcely
in it. That was it, my life's high point,
from which I thought an overflow of joy
would stream far down to water arid years…
that miracle of such excess, some said
it was waste. Who knows? Perhaps it was:
the wine unending splashing on the tables
of the feast and later, as our drinking
deepened, the dusty earth herself consumed it.
Spilled vessels, careless pours… what I
would give now for one of those lost drops!

It's twelve years ago, that wedding day.
And see me now: an infant son long buried,
a husband newly gone. The day is nothing,
a story from another life.

                                       I see
it still: the look he wore when the steward
whispered in his ear, the look of shame,
the look that over years became his face
and then I felt for the first time the certain
special anguish of a wife whose husband
is ashamed. Then they went away,
and they came back, and there was wine, and much
more than we needed, and my love had still
his honor. Only later did he tell me
of what Mary's Son had done.

                                   I never
saw her after that, though I heard
of miracles, too many to recount.
Our son fell ill. We hoped that he would come.

But he did not, and then it was too late.
What kept us from asking him to come?
I think we thought we'd had our miracle.
I wonder, to this day I wonder: why
that miracle? Sure, the wine was good,
but in other towns the dead were raised.

I heard that he died too, Mary's son—
young, I think. His mother was so young.
I wonder if she also wondered why.

I have tried to wait in faith. Our fathers
in the desert had one sign to keep them
through the years; I had one tiny sign,
one sign that meant that God had eyes for me,
for all the small grapes growing on the hills;
for the pebble carried home at dusk;
for the first of my son's steps, and for
the last; for each loaf of new bread rising
on the stones; a little head asleep;
a joke beside the fire; an empty seat.

There was so much of it, that magic wine,
jars and jars of it, like blood pouring
from the altar I have never seen,
a great river coming down to flood
our stricken plain, bring crops and plenty,
bearing flowers in the spring. For years
I've fought to make my miracle suffice.
I've weighed it in the scales with my grief
and tried to make it balance. But at last
I say: the sign alone won't satisfy.
Water into wine is not enough.

Sestina for Mother

The sun creeps a little higher.
Around the house the air is cold.
Inside they are eating eggs,
as they always do. The glass
gives back their every breath as fog.
The floor is littered again with toys.

Time drags. The child toys
with his food. He complains, higher-
pitched than before. The fog
fades. Outside it is too cold
to play, but the sun through the glass
says otherwise. Now the eggs

are on the floor. Now the eggs
are in heaps. Now they are toys
of greatest interest. Now the glass
is smeared with eggs, and so much higher
than before—another cold
day. Time has passed, a fog

of days. Again like breath the fog
wipes the window, but now the eggs
are balanced on a spoon. They're cold
before the child's finished. The toys
find homes in shelf space, always higher.
Open handprints fog the glass,

eager. The days become like glass
and she gets glimpses through the fog:
the child's bright eyes higher
than her waist; the steaming eggs
devoured, the old garish toys
give way, and outside the cold

is not too fierce. Now that cold
world can be faced. A door of glass
rattles behind him. Now his toys
she does not understand. A new fog
billows up. She makes the eggs.
What else can she do? And higher

and higher; now he prepares the eggs.
She grips old days as toys in fog,
glass baubles against the cold.

The Trout

I plucked it from its lake, burning cold
smoke-haze rising from the silver surface
that imitates the sky. Now I hold
it, red-licked gills throbbing without purpose
beneath the curving ridge of the teeth, cupped
around the dark pass of the throat. Deep down
I'll find the iridescent guts, tight-packed
with amber roe, and the fillets crowned
with the mud vein. But first: it's got to die.
My father says, *You want it to be quick,*
and demonstrates the snap against the stone.
I grip it hard; there in the opaled eye
is all the sky above me; I grasp and flick;
the sky contracts, clouds, withdraws, unknown.

Collect: Pebbles on the Beach by the Puget Sound

for the Feast of St. Dunstan

O God, who art
at once revealed and concealed
in thy creation, I confess
that this beach of pebbles drives me
to despair and to the grave
sin of avarice, to an insatiable lust
for things with shape.
The older the beach—
the more sphered and worn the stones—
the harder the longing takes me.
I am made ravenous for their round,
their smooth,
their effortless embodiment
of abstractions
that makes them so like you (in whom,
I am told but do not grasp,
such accidents are essential),
abstractions that exist
in my mind, out of reach
but here in these stones
become, almost, things
themselves, near perfection.
I confess that I itch to gather
them all to myself,
to cup them in my hands, bury them
in my pockets and take them,
add them to the piles
on my windowsill,
my hutch, my bookshelf,
as if by bringing creation
into my home

bit by bit I will master it
and through it, its evident
and elusive Master.

Daybreak in Bretagne

None now of that sheer gold of sunset,
decadent, the clarity of last light
on scarlet poppies.

Now mist rides the muted fields like breath,
going out and at once returning. The dew
neither gathers itself nor dissipates.

The world herself is an aging nun, veiled
in gray but for the cool luminance
of her quiet face.

Post Partum

for Leo

See, along the path those clustered sword-like leaves?
Those are the irises, my son; in spring they send up
purple plumes like smoke or thunderheads sharp-split
by blades of yellow lightning. In spring the wet ground gashes
itself open round the stalks—if it could bleed,
it would, there where new growth marks places of parting.

But look, out to the north, the clouds are finally parting
(though it's too far for your young eyes to see). The leaves
are dripping in the garden, and the colors bleed
through the raindrops on the glass. I'll put up
the window so you can see what you can see: gashes
of white fenceposts, and beyond, the dark horizon, split

around those glowing posts. All things now are split
like that for me, for I have been the Red Sea parting
and I have been a pale pathway through it. The gashes
in the rock at Meribah are me, for I leave
scars upon myself, and the water drawn up
from the rock is also me. The roots of *bleed*

are in the lost word *bhel*: to bloom, blossom, bleed
out life in color and flame. The whole sense is split
between death and life. Even our words bind those two up
together… Oh at last: you've gone to sleep, parting
your lips, still sucking. Each moment of your waking leaves
you bewildered by this world that is not you, by the gashes

widening between you and what you know, gashes
opened first by God in the Creation, which still bleed,
plumy, spreading. The Welsh for *bloom* is *blawd*. Leaves
must peel outward from the tree. A seed must split.

So nature manifests the mystery of parting
from the beginning: *and God said,* and so divided up

everything. Creation changes everything: up
from one thing rises endless others. Being gashes
itself open on itself; the great parting
does not end. They say even God had to bleed
for it. Like you and me, the world's forever split
apart by being what it is, my son. Always, the leaves

pile up around the trees. Spotted tree trucks bleed
sap in spring. To live is to split open. Without gashes
there are no leaves. All places mark our place of parting.

Act of Poetry

It goes like this: a *pond* is like nothing
more than it is like that brimming O
between consonantal banks
a little muddied with spring rains,
and then a *stone* sits heavy on the tongue
in just the way it snugs in the hand,
and when the two meet,
there is nothing more like itself
than the hollow that opens briefly
in the water when the stone falls through,
the clearing left by the smack
of being against being, and into
that space where stone and pond
were both and are no longer
there rushes for a moment the *void*
whose edges hum with energy
but whose core is a limitless lack
of energy… then the act ends,
and the waters close again over the gap,
about which now it can be said
only that it may indeed have been nothing
or it may have been a stab
into everything.

White Lily

Mary's flower

A single calla lily rises, slight and pale,
from a cut-glass vase upon my table.

Why do people call these flowers white?
as white, perhaps, as waxy-cold storm light

driven just before the hail, as some
dim star whose atmospheric color runs

like slowly spreading paint; they're all the shade
of oil-tattered foam upon the waves.

I dare not call anything *white* at all,
or white *anything*. It is a puzzle. The whole

premise, the promise of it, is to be
nothing—no shade, no hue—discernably

more than any other thing, or rather
to be everything at once, together.

See that calla lily: see the pale green
sheath that curves along the spine, the sheen

upon the petal like the gloss of flesh
beating blue with blood. See the crushed

yellow spadix at the core and how
the color radiates, reflecting out

and up the flute. Such a simple flower,
comprehensible and neat, without

excess mystery… until I look, just there,
at the petal's very brim, at a span where

the greeny edge and yellow center meet,
crossed below with shaded veins, and *that*

is beginning to be white, the single
band where all colors meet and mingle

at their fullest, themselves ceasing not to be
present at the supernova heart of purity.

The New House

First rain in the new house—
walls passed inspection, but
who knows? It's hard to trust
in bricks. Aren't they just cut-up

mud, lashed now by spray
from clotted gutters?
At the ground, the water preys
thumb-deep. What's happening

downstairs? Do I want
to know? In the old house
my mother lay upstairs
on the old flower couch

dying—*that* was a storm,
bricks battered, cracked,
shingles torn and flung,
foundation stones scattered

and returned to earth.
Rain eating at the walls
but not from outside, no,
not from outside at all—

and when I couldn't stand it,
I went downstairs to where
the kids were playing Lego,
the sets I used to cherish.

My daughter, two, nestled
beside the drain
sunk in the floor, happily
clicking a few bricks

together and apart
and together and
apart, building and wrecking
in one and the same

creative act, her face
bright with the dreadful joy
of angels. While upstairs
the rain, the rain that buoys

and erodes, falls
and softens every bond,
every tissue, ligament,
tie of flesh and blood,

gone. What's happening
downstairs? I go below,
fumbling unfamiliar
switches. A sudden flood

of light. The concrete slab,
the white block walls, the whole
expanse that we imagine
finishing someday. And there is

a little water. Not much,
for now. I climb the stairs.
Sit at the cluttered table.
And outside, the rain.

To My Unborn Child
for Stella

There is a story of how God,
before anything else existed, was everything.
And one day he looked out and saw
that everything was him, and he knew
that if he wanted to make some other thing,
first he'd have to vacate
some of what is, to make room, you see.
And so (the story goes) he breathed
in a mighty breath and with it
he pulled in a little of himself,
leaving just the smallest hollow
surrounded by the everything
that is him. Then, into
the hollow, he breathed, but kept himself
held back, just a little, and in
that empty space he made all Creation.

I wish I knew, dear little one,
if the story is true, and if
now he sits like this, hands cupped
around the hollow at his center
that is filling up with something
that is not entirely him;
if he too feels it shift and kick,
and what it is he wonders then.

Church Cleaning

At midday I go to pray at the mission church
downtown, the one where a few years back
the priest was shot and died.

It's been redecorated: ceiling vaults of birch,
some rugged saints, the Stations pale and framed in black
as if the scarlet in the side

of the Crucifix, like the desert sun, erodes
the strength of everything else, even the colors.
The overhead lights are off,

but as usual I find Eve Marcos
is there to clean the church, just as on all other
Saturdays. I cough

to let her know I'm there. She smiles and sweeps
down every empty row. Then she genuflects
in front of the altar before she goes to mop

at the base of the Our Lady shrine. As the mop seeps
out her shining offering of water, the wet tiles reflect
another Mary, smiling, even softer

and more full of light. And as Eve passes
down the center aisle, gold-leaf stars shimmer
at her feet around the prismed faces

of the stained-glass saints. Masses
of color bloom underfoot till the ceiling itself is dimmer
than that humble floor. In the dark spaces

along the outer walls she moves now through the depths
of a mirrored Paradise. One by one
the Stations—five, six, seven—

appear in her train, and behind her footsteps
Christ falls again and again, only now
he falls upwards into the radiant heart of Heaven.

Watercolor

In the pond, water layers
like paint: nearest, a warming skin
of green and gold,
sinuous as a snake's back,
then farther down, a muscled brown
pulsing with the carps'
anguished coupling.
But even that is not the bottom…
the bottom, a vast
swatch of a color that cannot be seen
but only felt, as on the day
when the pond was drought-shrunk
and I jumped in and was caught
knee-deep in silky muck, down
where there pulses the sweaty tender
underarm, under-breast,
under-thigh of earth, and still,
long after human hands hauled me back
to the world of greens and browns,
I feel it sometimes beside me,
brushing my neck, my arm, invisible,
that other color—oxblood?
amaranth? rose madder?—no,
not any of them, but now I think I know,
at least a little, why
God had the temple veiled
the way He did; how Socrates chose
his favorite hue; what the bougainvillea's
playing at; I know what shade is there
beneath all others, and why,
against all reason, I long
to breathe deep the wine-dark sea.

The Circle

Without fail it starts by circling wide—
it's sizing up the prey.
My son and mother watch.
What's that? my son asks, pointing up
even as the circle tightens.

Sunlight sheers red through
my mother's unmuscled arms,
shaking with radiation sickness, bruises
like talon-marks on her neck
from my baby daughter's fingers.

My son's laugh rings out, and I'm deceived
into hope. But overhead,
the bird is still circling.
It has a vast patience, almost
infinite—almost, but not quite.

Harvesting Olives in Arcadia

Today we went out to harvest the olives,
and in the unexpected clarity of the air—
as if a sea breeze were breathing on our desert—
I heard for one moment gulls
crying beside the Aegean
above the briny voices of Greek grandpapas in mid-story;
and when I saw the fruit hanging
shy behind veils of white yeast,
I felt briefly the dismay of flocks of children
who, in the savage squander of youth,
have scaled the branches to grasp fistfuls
of wine-dark olives and bite, triumphant, into them,
only to find they are wells of bitterness—
more bitter than the salt sea beneath,
more bitter than the tears that bubble up and slip
unbidden into the corner of a mouth—
while far below the grandpapas laugh,
remembering their first stolen taste of olive,
and the grandmamas shake their kerchiefed heads
and do not look up from their slow work
of crushing each fruit gently
with the flat of a knife to break it and begin
to ooze the milk of bitterness out.

Hymn to an Open Box of Spaghetti as It Falls from the Pantry Shelf

If there is any Muse left to sing, O sing of this
strange cascade of gold that bursts like a spring waterfall
from that dusty corner of the pantry shelf!
Sing of its quick, vigilant sound
of fingers shirring on the tight skin
of a drum before the masked players enter the stage,
or of the mesmeric motion of a dark box tipping,
slowly tipping—it seems for an age—
until at last it spills its hoard
of fierce scattered bars of sunlight.

Was this how cold Danae, also alone
in the grey chamber of her thoughts, staggered
in surprise at the abrupt intrusion
of a torrent of being, of shock and crash
and battering out-flung brilliance?
Did she too by instinct stretch to catch it
and then lean back contented
on her heels and, for as long as the shower fell,
satisfy herself with gazing?

Surely this is how Apollo's gleaming arrows fell,
jubilantly and with vengeance
on those who did not venerate the holy in their midst—
see how the noodles shoot into shadowed corners,
down through gas burners, behind the stove,
searching out the hidden places
in which to shatter and remain, to remind me
when in days to come I find them,
that every interruption is a little bit death,
and a little bit beckoning back to life.

The School of Athens in the Sonoran Desert

That's where Diogenes
could live, in that barrel-
cactus, could grow fat
on gravel and reluctant
rain and count himself
no further from the truth
of life than in Athens; see
there, a lean cypress tree
indicates the sky with a single
Platonic index finger,
beside an olive bole spreading
its thick-veined branches
like an open palm.
In the middle of an endless, dry-
heated debate, they all agree:
there is some flourishing at least
to be done here.

Meanwhile far overhead,
cold air from the north
swirls through papery cirrus
clouds, tracing hectic blue
Heraclitean currents,
and in identical hundreds
winter geese again follow
 each other south,
neither coming nor going,
thick and lonely as the stars
crossing heaven on their own
unceasing pilgrimage home.

Overflow

Somewhere up the street, out of sight, someone
has left the irrigation siphon open again.

Now, far down, I dip my hand in the stream
and press my palm flat against the concrete gutter.

The water tugs cool and dark on my forearm,
and through it I see my fingers flecked with light,

sand swept along and sifting through them.
A dry leaf bobs past, clinging so completely

to the water's skin that its top is entirely dry; it rises
seamlessly around the solitary mountain

island that is my wrist and arm and shoulder.
I think of the irrigation manager somewhere

up the street, distracted—chatting with a neighbor,
having a smoke, or simply absorbed

in watching what he has released: the play of light
on ripples, roving deep in the bottomless dark

water at the mouth of the siphon—and I wonder
if it is better to think of the Creator as like him, or as more

like this swift-loosed flood, this quickening rush
bubbling up irretrievably to overflow.

Marco Polo

Every summer in these neighborhoods
where children play quick rounds of Marco Polo
across the continents and small seas
of their backyards and swimming pools,
when every neatly fenced afternoon dozes
and dreams of perilous quests to lost places,
there is always one small brown boy
whose sharp voice is stern beyond his years,
who shouts and skips at the searcher's very fingertips
because he knows that he is brave,
and knows the others know it too,
and knows that courage means nothing here,
who cuts with his body white silky roads
through the water that piles up continually
like little Himalayas between him and his companions,
who is the first to shout *Polo!*
and the first to spring back, at once—
like the hidden world he loves—
begging and refusing to be found.

Resurrection After a Headache

To be no longer tempted to succumb
to mindless panic that this is the one
that will not end, that this numb
agony means at last I am done
with the simple thing called Health, that ballast
state in which no part disrupts the quiet
whole, for that is how we love our lancing
flesh the best: by dwelling not on it.

And yet, after the headache comes the creaking
joy of recognition: ah, frail unwhole,
it's you! Eyes not throbbing with the gallant
light; keen awareness of throat calling
I am coming—I, body, in which soul
has stumbled, caught itself, and once more balanced.

Icon of Elijah in the Wilderness

Next door there's a playhouse
up in a grapefruit tree,
like a cave among the branches.
This evening a gold-leaf sunset
burns between the boards
like sky on a Byzantine icon.
The ladder's pulled up,
and in the corner
the little hermit hunkers
on his heels, his blue t-shirt
just visible. Down the darkening
street through open doors
drift voices, music,
neon of televisions,
but the tree is a grotto
of silence and little winds.
Evening creeps up
and purples the world
so sound and perspective
bend round on themselves
and cars on the distant
freeway seem as close
as the lovebirds chattering
in the palm fronds overhead.
Only the noisy lit interiors
of other people's houses
are far away and strange. Someone
calls from a back door, outlined
against flashes from a screen,
but in the cave set high
in the grapefruit tree, all is still,
so still the pigeons begin
to settled down for the night
among the waxy leaves

above the little hermit's head,
and by the movement
of their wings knock fruit,
sun-warmed, to roll on the floor
up to his quiet feet.

The Fig

Just last week I found
the year's first fig nestled,
almost ripe,
behind vast, luminous leaves
that held back the light
the way a mother's arm
by instinct curls out
and scoops her small son up
into a gentle embrace
when he runs past her laughing
on his way to see
what he should not see
just yet.

Leap

One night along the path I come
upon a rabbit, wounded, lamed,
his one bright eye a vast of black
around a single star, head bent, back
broken, but sleek forelegs still
rampant, pumping in a final
splendid frolic all alone,
the mighty hindlegs inert and bone
thrusting from the fur, and still
the great forelegs leap on, milling
the whole little body in an arc
upon the ground all dark
with blood, and still those legs
leap on, springing as the muscles beg
for life, for movement learned
and learned and by time burned
into those sinews that begin to still,
but, as the single star dims, will
still, unto the very end, leap on.

Sonnet for Early Autumn

To all appearances it's summer still—
blooms still lace these vines, the polished sky's
still bright above leafed trees. The sunlight lies
in vivid strips along the windowsill.

And yet, there's something different to it all.
Some dream is done. The shadows have a sudden
chill that full sun can't dispel. I glimpse, hidden
within this fertile place (and not too well)

vague indications of decay: an aching
limb, a trackless pang, freshness wilting
quietly, and everywhere that obscure
weariness, the huddling up, the bracing
against the trickling wind, the careful tempering
of a heart that was so quick, so sure.

In the Sandbox

for Leo and Stella

Sand sifting through
and over your fingers:
that is power enough,
for you know that to build

is to be divine
in this small world.
By your spoon and single
truck, you are deified,

as good as any god-
king or queen of old
Mesopotamia, steering
a kingdom of clay.

~ ~ ~

Scoop and dump, you whisper,
and you scoop, and dump,
and down roll the spheres,
countless tumbled grains

of primeval stuff: cold clay;
quartz; volcanic black
basalt torn up from
earth's heart; they all fall

at your feet, side by side
with limestone from lost seas,
the pale, crushed tomb
of some ancient water-life.

~   ~   ~

Child's-play: the saying is
it's easy. Sure, as easy as
creation, but no easier.
Easy as invention, generation;

easy as mothering, stewarding,
construction, irrigating,
hunting, fishing, planting
reaping; easy as persuasion,

bartering, marshalling
and dispersing; easy
as peace, but more difficult
by far than war.

~   ~   ~

You scoop, and dump.
You raise towers, not quite
to heaven, but to its toes.
Your task is great,

and the small shovel quakes.
The sand dances on the rim,
held only by the imperious gravity
of your young face, dancing

on the rim of being, even as meteors
ring this grave world, itself only a grain
tipped long ago and falling still
from a bright and innocent cup.

Making Peace with the Cat

See her walk the room, an enigmatic
slip as opulent as black velvet
lingerie, frivolous but magnetically
composed.
               Her narrow face, delicate
upon a liquid neck, and then, her body,
all swing and swaying motion tucked in snug
beneath her collected muscles.
                                 Her haughty
Eyes are fixed on something—sofa? rug?
sunlit hardwood floor?—beside my feet.

She does not look at me, and I am flattered,
for she only permits her gaze to rest
on things unmoving, inanimate, concrete—
soulless things that cannot look back.
She avoids me. Thus, I have passed some test.

Still Life with Dead Jackdaw

A grub-chewed ornamental eggplant bush
sprawls, discarded, in the alley, rootless
as Yggdrasil at the end of days—
the worm poison got it just as surely
as the worms would have.
Yellow eggplants languish in the dust
like little worlds; they don't realize yet
their universe is overthrown.
Ripening purple floods
down longitudinal lines from the north pole
of the largest to its swelling equator,
which has been pecked open—split
as if there's a rip in the ocean.
Seeds flood out, and inside it is full of ants.
I don't see the jackdaw caught
in the *rigor mortis* of the stems
until I pick the bush up by its base
and the glossy little corpse hops
to the ground by my foot. I flinch away
but he bounces after me
on the iron-hard dirt, as if
he was only playing at being dead
and was ready to go on forever that way,
head cocked and merry black eyes fixed
on his trove of poisoned treasure.

My Children Gather Acorns

In bright October, my children gather acorns.
My mother's birthday would have been next week.
She dreaded cold; every year she mourned
in bright October. My children gather acorns—
they do not know what comes. To them, the shorn
winter's just a game, a mythic freak
in bright October. My children, gather acorns.
My mother's birthday would have been next week.

Penelope

Again the house is quiet, as in the early
days when he first left, before the suitors
came. Again, the mid-day moves as gently
as the early morning. His vast oars
have beat the waves one final time. The chill
wind is still. The house, the docks below,
the scepter and the isle—all are still
here. Only he is not.   I know
what they will say: that he abandoned me
again in my old age, that I could not
keep him. Envy, mistrust, loneliness,
all fierce passions tangle in the knot
of marriage—mine was no exception. I say
mine, for it was mine. Is mine. Remains
mine. He had no part in it, save
what I lent to him and now reclaim…
or rather, as he lets it fall, receive.
For I am always there, like this shore,
and every wave that leaves these shores leaves
a little of itself behind.   Sure,
he dreamt of other bodies, lithe, smooth-limbed,
those goddesses, supple-eyed and steely,
sporting in his arms like fish and him,
my Odysseus, my king, kneeling
at their naked feet.   He thinks he left them
to return to me, but I know better.
That man's never left a thing, only been
sent away, and summoned, and then sent
away again by those who love him but
desire him no more.   And now he's gone,

taken his old ships and men and bent
his eyes west, away, from the dawn,
from Troy, Calypso (yes, I learned her name),
from his wanderings, from the Ithaca
he said he loved. This quiet. It's the same
as before, or rather, what it was
before was what it is now. Like me.
For I, Penelope, have not changed.
That is my virtue, isn't it? To be
exactly what I am. Always to range
the hills and valleys of myself and not
to strive to seek to find what is beyond.

But then, unlike him, I can plot
myself on a map. I am becalmed,
sure, but I know where I am: here,
in Ithaca. What he desired, I
became: the rocks, the ragged hills, the clear
horizon arching overhead, the dry
wind that shakes and rattles in the doorposts
of our home. Aged we are, yes,
withered, cragged. Floods have torn our coasts.
Each year the harvest is a little less.
And yet, what we are, we are: the same,
the very same when he leaves us as when
he fought down gods and men to return, claim
us as his own. The sea moans again;
again, the wind. I am Ithaca,
which will not be vanquished by the sea.
I am Ithaca, as always was;
as still is; as he could never be.

The Lark Ascending Over Phoenix

I saw one evening a lark ascending
on air, unburdened by all but love
of rising. Such a thing you cannot see
too many times. It is a feast of movement
hallowing each moment, at once rising
and suspended, by swiftness stilled.

I return to this instant as a composer
returns in a theme to the same note,
which does not insist upon itself
but is simply there, until it has become
something beyond itself. The note
returns and is richer. The lark toys
with his ascension, and without reason
I recall to mind the abandoned shore
I walked at daybreak long ago,
and the empty city street gleaming
in the rain, and the hour spent alone
in a stone church at twilight, or the night

years ago in a small room open to the sky
when I saw the dance of the whirling dervishes
beneath the stars on the high, cold plains
of Anatolia, and now the lark remembered
calls to mind how that dance begins:
in a soft twist of white skirts, billowing
out, swift shifting, swirling, filling
with movement like kites with wind
till the dancers are flying, flying in place,
and all the time their sky-blue caps are still,
fixed firm as pin-heads in a cushion
while the white skirts circle around them
and every movement only adds to the stillness.

On cloudless days I can go outside,
look up, and begin to turn, faster and faster,
till all the world is turning with me
except the sky, which is fixed fast above me
as blue ink in white cloth, which does not move
in response to movement.

                      So it is
with the lark ascending. Some things cannot be
known. To reveal themselves, they bring to mind
the very things they are not. So music
can invoke silence, and movement
can mean stasis. A word spoken
can recall the very stillness it has broken,
to which all words return. Just so I return
to the moment one evening when the lark dropped,
dropped, and turned to rise again.

Explanation

It's because of the motion of the sun, or
it's because of the shadow of the earth, or
it's because of that pesky elliptical path it travels
that we always see the same side of the moon.
The other side has pressing business elsewhere.
But just you try explaining that to a child
when he learns that something (dread? or lovely?)
is always turned away from him, like an eye
with only the white showing, an eye forever
rolled back into the socket of the heavens.
Try responding when he wonders what the other side
of the moon is looking at so attentively.
Try answering when he asks what would happen
if one night, overhead, its vast pupil roved into view.

Words and Pictures

Billboards in Times Square and an exhibit of medieval illuminated Scriptures at the Metropolitan Museum of Art

Otherworldly, this fresco above
                    the marbled floor, the mingling interplay of
the Square. No one can at first resist
                    color and un-color, how the twisting
vision all around, sharp as fire
                    greenish serpentine and ruddy iron
rising up the walls of this place,
                    coil to the base of the glass case
flickering around the silhouettes,
                    where lie the ancient books, with their yet-
young faces, beautiful and blank, that blaze
                    distinct letters, dutiful in praise
huge in signs and screens, enraptured, lit
                    from within neat-measured borders, writ
with all the fervor the young only bear
                    with precise desperation, each line a prayer
for themselves. Vast electric eyes
                    like a spear flung through the dark that flies
in appeal to heaven, which is somewhere near
                    straight and true before it disappears
in the upper limits of the screen.
                    But around the words and in between
the massive pupils gape: there, sure,
                    blossoms the whole world in miniature:
light that's stripped of *Kingdom Animalia's*
                    red and green and golden marginalia,
so mutable nature—a lifeless light begun
                    where a monstrous rabbit pursues a nun,
before the world and time, begun where
                    teeth bared, the nun is laughing; here,

pure intelligences reign, unkind
                        to a man—shoved by a griffin from behind—
before the invention of matter and of love
                        goes flailing into barnyard muck. Above,
perfect things shatter before cute
                        nuns who, laughing, harvest obscene fruit,
o absurdity! by you God snuffs
                        through a tree of butts and dangling nuts
out that lifeless light that does not bend
                        below, where a tiny knight defends
words against the reality that rails—
                        the letter "I" among a troop of snails—
against and through them: words, prisoners
                        with human heads and paws of taloned tigers
in pulsing pink, purple, blue, relentless,
                        this world around the words still luminous,
a blazing green, red, orange, crude,
                        so bright it's hard to tell: which is the jewel—
fierce pictures that keep their truth absurd
                        and which the setting—those silent, watchful
                        words.

Down the Basement Stairs

In my old house the overhead fixture shed light
down to the landing, but from that point, the descent
sank into infernal shades, and when at night

I, unlucky, chose the short straw and was sent
to fetch cards, a game, some ice cream from the freezer,
I'd skulk there on that landing, for to pass it meant

to creep through shadows, risking always being seized
by wrist or ankle and hauled relentless down the final stairs
through the black door that flexed and gaped as if it breathed.

And, if I made it, at the bottom was despair,
for then I'd plunge my arm into the harrowing
abyss and grope blindly for the light switch. There

on those stairs I learned mortality is a thing
with teeth: we're all born bitten. You can't outrun
the shapeless dark. To this day I feel it, the nothing

at my heels as when, my task complete, I'd run
back to the lighted landing, the domain in between
where shadows stayed pinned in place and the one

light kept back—for now—the darkness waiting there,
still crouching, silent, claws sharp, eyes keen, teeth bare.

Winter Scene

Ink-black, the trees are calligraphy
against a mute sky, lines
of a strange script.

Around the water's edge an icy
stillness spreads, catching frail designs
where snowmelt has dripped.

Each mallard moves away, encased
in his own inescapable ring of ripples,
inhabiting his delicate tension.

Part

Another departure: papa leaves again
for work. Once again our little son
obediently shuts the door of glass
then stands at it and weeps.

Repetition is no consolation.
His five hundred days of life
have not yet wrung a pattern
out of this relentless parting.

So every day behind his clear barrier
he cries and with a finger traces
on the fogged glass the history of loss
in dripping hieroglyphics.

He doesn't see, yet there is a pattern—
entropy, after all, is in its own way
predictable. Everything scatters
into its discrete parts, doesn't it?

Years ago I stood at the altar
beside an other, and since then
we have tried—oh how we've tried—
to press these fragments together

into a whole, all the while
knowing it's just a matter of time
till death do us and all
our many pieces part.

And repetition is no consolation,
not for me, not for my mother
who is dwindling before an ancient cancer.
What's Eriugena say? *Do you not see*

how the Founder of the whole universe
holds the first place in division?
As if that's supposed to help,
that God is better than us even at pain.

How many times has she seen this
inevitable ending played out? First a sister,
then beloved friends, and every time it is new,
and repetition is no consolation.

It's always troubled me, that mystery
of the Ascension, the Divine coming
and going casual as a morning visit,
always promising he'll be back.

How long, I wonder, did the disciples stand
there, gazing up at the glass sky
slammed shut, tracing his shoulders
in the hieroglyphic clouds?

I go out for a walk one evening
in the last of the freezing light
that spills out bloody from the sun split
on the black edge of the earth.

Jupiter is overhead, and Mars
coming up behind the sunset.
From across the water I hear
laughter in our little house.

The ice on the pond cracks, and dark water
slips by—coming or going,
I cannot say—like the fleet foot
and bended back of God.

Ponds

The last words of Theoderic the Ostrogoth to his magister, Cassiodorus

So, Cassidorus, it is you.
And just how long have you been standing there
in the shadows, cloaked in your dark habit
of silence? You wear it so easily,
even after all these years—but then
you have always wielded silence as a weapon
against me, Theoderic, king
of the Ostrogoths and of Rome,
though it is by me the walls still stand
around Byzantium and your beloved Rome.

I know you recall that day
when at table I struck down Odoacer,
the rat-faced general from Ravenna,
my rival for the throne. It's true,
we'd pledged peace, but it was putrid from the start…
what could I do but strike first?

How you, in all your learning,
looked with such disdain at the blood
that sprinkled the meat of the feast!
You condemned me then, Cassiodorus,
but you never were a king.
You never wept as you heard the crash
when Roman towers shattered like glass,
nor saw the showers of soul-sparks rise
when the hammer of God struck the anvil of the pride
of men outside the gates of Byzantium.
You did not mark where your arrows fell
on the very doorstep of the pit of Hell,
nor did you, wading through the blood of tribes,
take and wield, for the last time,

the Roman law as a burning brand
against the monstrous night.

I did all this, and more besides.
I knew, my boy, what you did not:
that there is a noble living to be made
in the brutal defense of something good
that you have not lived by, or even understood.
Now your philosophy molders away
in a mildewed chest somewhere in Italy
behind walls I gave my soul to save,
while over every door there gleams
a token of old Rome's glory,
and mark my words: by that gleam
the night may yet pass us by.

I know what you are going to say;
the night passes no one by.
All this life, you say, is merely
the making of oneself into a candle
to burn with God's light into the dark
that comes, relentless, to us all.
Don't say it. I know
what comforts your kind brings
to the deathbed of a failed king;
your silence is doubtless the gentlest thing.

My curse is I was born
just when I was, at a joint in time,
and lived a man between the days,
a man whom all other ages
point at, and mock, and will not understand.
Today it is not permitted to be
simply a barbarian lord. That
has its own nobility to it. But I became
something worse, something tawdry:
a peddler of tame superstitions,
a seller of trinkets and pedantries,

haggling in villages over bastardized Latin,
shreds of theology, scraps of philosophy,
the baubles and bangles of civilization
stripped from her still-warm corpse and hawked
in the marketplace as her bridal jewels.
What do I truly know of wisdom?
What tools did I have to divine
the nature of the Incarnation,
whether Christ was made man or whether
his was a greater mystery than being made?
How could I hope to plumb the secret
space that hangs between sound and silence,
the two voices of God? And yet
to rightness in all this will I be held,
in this life and in the one to come.

What a strange thing is life,
and small! Look: the clouds hang low,
and we will soon have rain.

Do you remember that long spring
when for weeks the rain up-country
fell and befouled the river with mud?
Ah, and you were always laboring
at building your useless little ponds,
even on days when the frost still clung
at dawn to the soil, those fish-ponds to which
you wanted to bring (you said) the river
as it ought to have been.
                                        I saw them
later, in summer, full. Such ponds!
As clear, cool, quiet as jewels,
brimming with shadows and light, with motion
and stillness, and the very sounds they made
were silence.
                Then I thought that those
must be the happiest of fish,
darting through limpid water beneath

the crested stalks of the water-flowers,
to them the mightiest of pillars
supporting the heaven of the water-surface.

Yes, the happiest of fish they were,
and, seeing them, I the happiest of men.
What a strange thing is life. Look: the clouds
hang low, and soon we will have rain.
But whether it will churn up or wash away
the mud, I cannot say.
                          Go, boy. Go
to your ponds. I know you are longing
to. Go. Yes, what a little thing
is life, and littlest of all its passing,
a raindrop's ripple on the water
stirring up reflections of clouds,
sky, a pink-budding locust tree
ruffled by the breeze. I find
some solace in that breeze; perhaps still,
as over the surface of your ponds,
in the stillness to which I go, it moves.

Evening Meditation

Such a risk you took
and are always taking—
to show yourself through beauty
so pristine it entices me to look
no further than itself,
to manifest yourself
in a world of such radiance
that I, seeing it,
am very nearly content
without seeing you.

Acknowledgements

After the Funeral - *First Things*

New Year's Morning - *Euphony Journal*

Saint January - *Ekstasis*

Pomegranate - *The New Ohio Review*

Candles - *The Windhover*

Spring Evening - commissioned by Chris Krycho and set to music

The Newlywed - *The Classical Outlook*

Relics - *The St. Katherine Review*

Annunciation - *Society of Classical Poets*

Sestina for Mother - *Fare Forward*

The Trout - *Able Muse*

Daybreak in Bretagne - *Ekstasis*

Post Partum - *Measure Review*

The New House - *Image Journal*

Church Cleaning - *Dappled Things*

Watercolor - *The Hopkins Review*

Hymn to an Open Box of Spaghetti as It Falls from the Pantry Shelf - *Convivium*

Overflow - *Plough Quarterly*

Marco Polo - *Fare Forward*

Resurrection After a Headache - *Mezzo Cammin*

In the Sandbox - *North American Anglican*

Still Life with Dead Jackdaw - *Euphony Journal*

Penelope - *The Hopkins Review*

Down the Basement Stairs - *Presence Journal*

Ponds - *The Lamp Magazine*

The Poiema Poetry Series

COLLECTIONS IN THIS SERIES INCLUDE:

Six Sundays Toward a Seventh by Sydney Lea
Epitaphs for the Journey by Paul Mariani
Within This Tree of Bones by Robert Siegel
Particular Scandals by Julie L. Moore
Gold by Barbara Crooker
A Word In My Mouth by Robert Cording
Say This Prayer into the Past by Paul Willis
Scape by Luci Shaw
Conspiracy of Light by D.S. Martin
Second Sky by Tania Runyan
Remembering Jesus by John Leax
What Cannot Be Fixed by Jill Pelaez Baumgaertner
Still Working It Out by Brad Davis
The Hatching of the Heart by Margo Swiss
Collage of Seoul by Jae Newman
Twisted Shapes of Light by William Jolliff
These Intricacies by David Harrity
Where the Sky Opens by Laurie Klein
True, False, None of the Above by Marjorie Maddox
The Turning Aside anthology edited by D.S. Martin
Falter by Marjorie Stelmach
Phases by Mischa Willett
Second Bloom by Anya Krugovoy Silver
Adam, Eve, & the Riders of the Apocalypse anthology edited by D.S. Martin
Your Twenty-First Century Prayer Life by Nathaniel Lee Hansen
Habitation of Wonder by Abigail Carroll
Ampersand by D.S. Martin
Full Worm Moon by Julie L. Moore
Ash & Embers by James A. Zoller

The Book of Kells by Barbara Crooker
Reaching Forever by Philip C. Kolin
The Book of Bearings by Diane Glancy
In a Strange Land anthology edited by D.S. Martin
What I Have I Offer With Two Hands by Jacob Stratman
Slender Warble by Susan Cowger
Madonna, Complex by Jen Stewart Fueston
No Reason by Jack Stewart
Abundance by Andrew Lansdown
Angelicus by D.S. Martin
Trespassing on the Mount of Olives by Brad Davis
The Angel of Absolute Zero by Marjorie Stelmach
Duress by Karen An-hwei Lee
Wolf Intervals by Graham Hillard
To Heaven's Rim anthology edited by Burl Horniachek
Cup My Days Like Water by Abigail Carroll
Soon Done with the Crosses by Claude Wilkinson
House of 49 Doors by Laurie Klein
Hawk and Songbird by Susan Cowger

"Billboards in Times Square converse with medieval illuminated manuscripts. A mother observes her child's incomprehension of patterns—movements of sun and moon, a father's departure for and return from work—as she stands outside the ongoing *now* he inhabits. The archangel Gabriel steps out of the timeless universe to kneel, in a single time and place, before a woman whose finite body will contain the infinite. With a formal restraint that tempers their heartfelt impulses, a historicity that holds the past in tension with the present they probe, Jane Scharl's poems engage with time and point to eternity."

—Sally Thomas,
co-editor of *Christian Poetry in America since 1940: An Anthology*

"Jane Clark Scharl has already distinguished herself in the verse drama. Now she makes her debut as a lyric poet with poems that partake of the same energy and curiosity, intertwining the religious, historical, and personal. The poet has a restless love of forms, with one poem sequence extinguishing light after light as it follows the pattern of a traditional Tenebrae service. Dramatic monologues free Scharl from the conventions of confessional, decentering the self in favor of the sublime as her questing faith keeps 'rising like a star / above the fretted seas of what had been.' A multitalented writer to watch."

—Amit Majmudar,
author of *Twin A: A Memoir*

"This is a fine book. Jane Clark Scharl's poems, in well-crafted free and formal verse, show us a world covered in light, often gentle but sometimes glaring. In its glow, we see common things (water, leaves, children, mothers) as if they had just been called into being."

—Burl Horniachek,
editor of *To Heaven's Rim: The Kingdom Poets Book of World Christian Poetry*

"Jane Clark Scharl's *Ponds* is a reminder of what poetry can be. Her starting points in the daily world are familiar to everyone—family, friends, nature, and worship. She quickly vaults to the universal world in ways reminiscent of Gerard Manley Hopkins, but with spare, precise language and rhythms closer to the best work of Thomas Merton. *Ponds* is a book to reread and savor."

—A. M. Juster,
poetry editor, *Plough*

"Jane Clark Scharl does something remarkable here. These highly crafted poems often approach the minimalism and tranquility of haiku—yet they're also like thoroughbreds collected under tight rein, bursting with the vigor of surprising-but-inevitable language. It's quite a feat."

—Jane Greer,
author of *Love Like a Conflagration*

"Jane Clark Scharl's mature and wonderful first book, *Ponds*, has mastered the art of saying less as a way of saying more. Scharl's work combines formal restraint with a full-bodied feel for the sensuous pulse of life. In these deeply intelligent, searching poems, Scharl accepts that 'some things cannot be known' but knows, too, that to reveal themselves, 'they bring to mind/the very things they are not.' Her poems are such revelations."

—Robert Cording,
author of *In the Unwalled City*

www.ingramcontent.com/pod-product-compliance
Lightning Source LLC
Chambersburg PA
CBHW022123040426
42450CB00006B/819